This book belongs to

_____

This book is dedicated to my children - Mikey, Kobe, and Jojo.

Copyright © 2022 Grow Grit Press LLC. All rights reserved. No part of this book may be reproduced in any form without permission in writing from the publisher. Please send bulk order requests to growgritpress@gmail.com

Paperback ISBN: 978-1-63731-597-2
Hardcover ISBN: 978-1-63731-599-6

Ninja Life Hacks®
by Mary Nhin

Printed and bound in the USA.
NinjaLifeHacks.tv

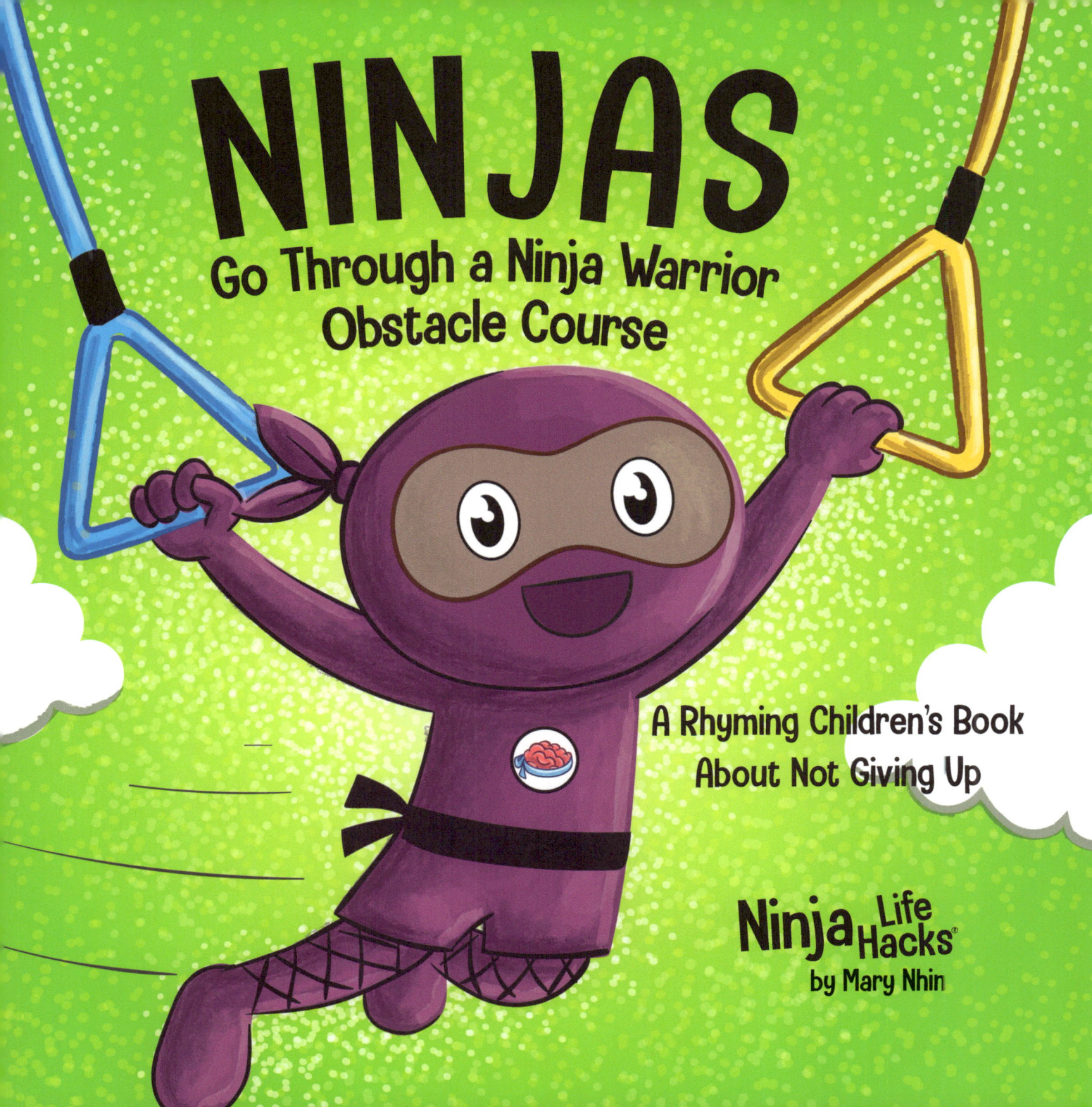

As part of a ninja's special training,
One thing they have to do
Is face the Ninja Warrior Obstacle Course,
And make it the whole way through.

I stood at the starting line.
It looked so far to the end.
But if I didn't try, I would never know,
On that I could depend.

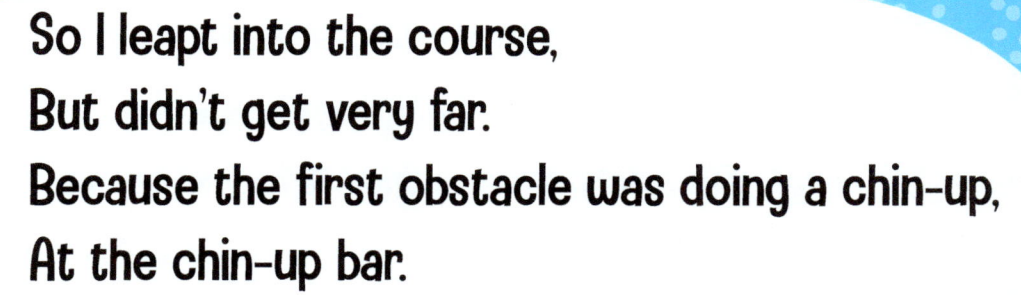

So I leapt into the course,
But didn't get very far.
Because the first obstacle was doing a chin-up,
At the chin-up bar.

Onto the chin-up bar I leapt,
And I didn't just do one.
I'd been practicing so very hard all week,
I did extra chin-ups for fun.

The next few obstacles weren't so bad.
Then came the hardest of all.
Seventeen ninjas had already failed
The slippery climbing wall.

I watched other ninjas try,
And learned from what I'd seen.
"It's hard to do this alone," I said,
"So let's climb the wall as a team!"

Up and over the ninjas all went,
And I was feeling great.
But I knew at the end of the obstacle course,
The jelly pond lay in wait.

It looked scary and sticky and wobbly as well,
You had to leap over in one.
I stared and said,
"I don't think that it can be done."

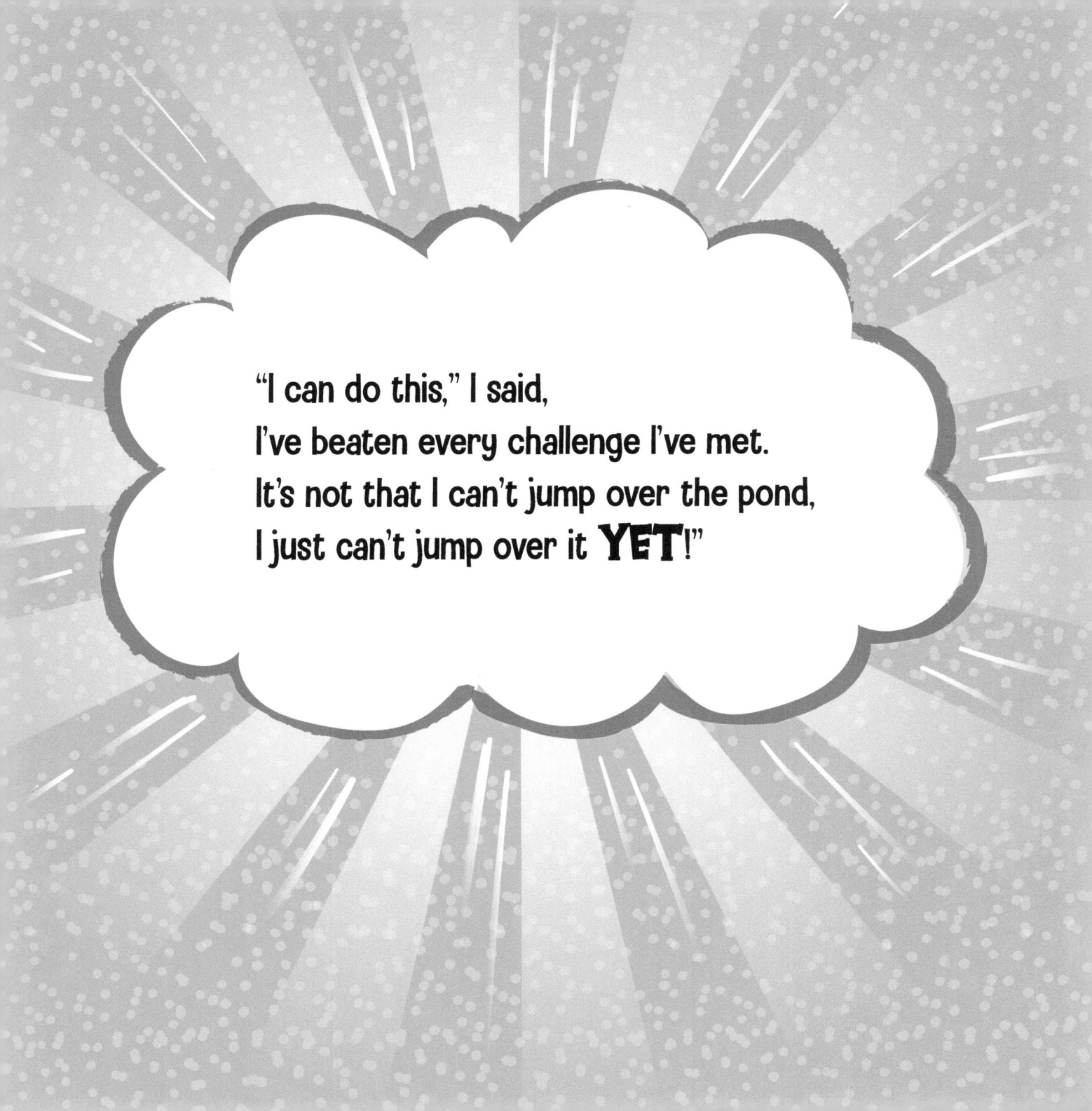

The other ninjas cheered and clapped and roared,
They loved how I never gave in.
And with a final try, the jelly was cleared,
It was little ol' me for the win!

I love to hear from my readers. Write to me at info@ninjalifehacks.tv and let me know your ideas for my next book!

Yours truly, Mary Nhin

 @marynhin @officialninjalifehacks  Ninja Life Hacks
#NinjaLifeHacks

 Mary Nhin   Ninja Life Hacks    @officialninjalifehacks

www.ingramcontent.com/pod-product-compliance
Lightning Source LLC
Chambersburg PA
CBHW041106070526
44583CB00002B/77